Best wishes,
Owen Hughes

TASMANIA

Island of Tranquillity

Dawn on the jetty at Freycinet Lodge, Coles Bay.

TASMANIA
Island of Tranquility

Photographs by OWEN HUGHES
Text by BERNICE JURGEIT
Book Design by OWEN HUGHES

'GREEN GABLES'

PUBLISHED & DISTRIBUTED BY OWEN HUGHES
17 Elizabeth Street, Launceston, Tasmania 7250, Australia. Telephone: (03) 6331 1481
http://www.owenhughes.com.au/

First Published 2004
Reprinted 2008

Typeset by Computer Support Tasmania, Lilydale, Tasmania, 7268, Australia
Map of Tasmania © Copyright TASMAP
Colour separation, printing & binding: Dai Nippon Printing Co. Printed in Singapore.

National Library of Australia ISBN number: 0-9590145-4-3

Ben Lomond dominates the breaking morning over farm land at Epping Forest on the Heritage Highway south of Launceston.

Foreword

By Dr Harry Cooper BVSc M.R.C.V.S.

Having spent the first 29 years of his life in a farming community on the east coast of Tasmania, Owen Hughes had the time and the perfect setting to reflect on why this island called Tasmania is the most picturesque state in the whole of Australia. It is now some twenty years since those reflections found their way via the art of photography to a book entitled quite sincerely, 'For the Love of Tasmania'.

There have been other volumes since but Owen has spent over two long years to ensure this is the best ever. He is excited by the pictures. The diversity of this special place is captured in images that range from the morning mists on the upper Derwent river to the aerial panorama of the Freycinet Peninsula, the thrill of the penny farthing races at Evandale to the quiet serenity of the wilderness high country.

It is a photographic tour of Tasmania, from ground level and from above. Here there is history, both man made and natural. Historic buildings with their tragic past contrast with modern city vistas. Even more imposing and far older is the record engraved by nature itself, starkly sculptured in a mountain range, but often inscribed on something as simple as the trunk of a tree.

The island too has its moods and these can change in a matter of seconds. Patience, perseverance and basically getting there at just the right time are only a part of the photographer's art. There have been lots of early mornings and many disappointments in the making of this book. The pages reflect the reverence Owen has for his home, the feeling that the world may be a wondrous place but coming home is the best part. As he so simply relates; here in a small corner of the world, a man is at peace within.

Contents

Acknowledgements

Special thanks to my wife Marcia for her understanding and patience.

Dr. Harry Cooper for the kind words in his foreword.

To all those who were involved in the production of this book.

The beach at Binalong Bay near St. Helens is popular with families at holiday time.

Surf fishing at Swimcart Beach in the Bay of Fires Coastal Reserve.

The Pilot Station at Low Head, established in 1805, marks the entrance to the Tamar River with George Town in the background. The present buildings date from 1835 and are open to the public seven days a week.

8

INTRODUCTION

Islands around the world captivate people with the promise of enchantment, sentiment and mystery. Tasmania, set adrift from the south-east coast of mainland Australia by the rise of ancient waters and held at the mercy of the temper of the Southern Ocean, is no exception to this promise. A small land mass of 68,331 square kilometres embedded in one of the roughest seas on earth, the island beckons discovery with its physical beauty and charm.

Wild country of pre-historic quartz ridges fall away to scalloped beaches of soft laid sands. Mountain ranges tower over fluted cliffs raised sentinel above the hinterland of rolling woodland and farms, dotted over with tiny towns. Tucked away beneath the 40th line of latitude the seasons are distinctly marked here with warm blue summer days easing in to autumn in a brilliance of fiery colour. With the waning days mist shrouds the lowlands while snow on the peaks drapes heavily above the dripping rainforests. From August the air cools before spring bursts through in dramatic fashion. Pink blossom dusts the trees in many country streets, daffodils cheerily sway in the waking winds and the rivers and creeks babble merrily with the flow of snow melt.

Home to one of the oldest races in the world, the Tasmanian Aboriginal, their simple culture made a sharp contrast with the technologies and skills of the European settlers. The landscape bears witness to these earliest inhabitants whose heritage remains etched into the land through cave paintings and rock carvings. Today's population reflects the cultural clashes between the colonial opportunists and indigenous people with descendants returning to traditional ways. The north eastern islands of Cape Barren and Flinders are home to many Aboriginal descendants who choose to adopt a more customary lifestyle.

Tasmania's rich colonial history overlays the natural landscape with Georgian architecture crafted in sandstone grandeur and humble convict brick, liberally represented in the cities and smaller towns. From wealthy rulers and merchants to the labourers and convicts of the 19th century, a robust trade in quality antiques continues to reveal the life of earlier settlers and a violent penal system. The curious will find many treasures pocketed in tiny shops in both town and country eager to share a story. Many historic homes now provide an enchanting accommodation option for visitors extending across the far reaches of the state.

Modern artisans inspired by the history and beauty of the landscape, draw on this resource to produce some of the finest art, literature, theatre and craft work in the world. Local glass and ceramics, fine art and print media, textiles, sculpture, dance, music and literature originate from the studios of shy hillside retreats and the vibrant life of larger towns and cities. While works can be found in galleries in most cities, the weekend country markets are the perfect place to find quality crafts and artworks at inexpensive prices.

Adventure is sought by many in the wild terrain of Tasmania's national parks. Walking tracks thread the mountain country attracting bush walkers and rafters. The natural landscape is a haven for native species of birds and mammals including quolls, wallabies and the Tasmanian Devil. Wildflowers carpet the ground in the warmer seasons with many species unique to the island. Marine parks along the coast line provide havens for fish, anemones and kelp forests bringing a rainbow of colour to the sea floor. Inland lakes are full with brown trout seasonally attracting anglers with small boats and fly rods.

Insulated yet innovative, Tasmania produces a paradoxical mix of inspired industry. Wooden boat building and furniture making draw on the natural forest for specialty timber. Fine merino wool traditionally sold on for bulk export, is now also spun into quality knitted or wool denim clothing. Native flowers have found a niche as commercially grown cut flowers for overseas markets, while the cool temperate climate has borne the fruit, literally, of the flourishing Tasmanian wine industry. Served in restaurants and cafes in cosmopolitan style, home grown, premium beef and dairy produce are complemented with the natural flavour of wild spice gathered from native plants.

Primary industry draws on coastal waters for oyster and salmon farming. Wild fisheries support a lucrative trade in crayfish, scale fish and abalone, serving local and overseas restaurants. Onions, potatoes, peas and grain grown on rich agricultural land, supply interstate markets together with apples, cherries and berry fruits. Niche markets have seen the rise of organic farms growing medicinal herbs and salad vegetables. Poppies colour the warm summer months on many farm paddocks to supply the pharmaceutical industry.

Yet, there still remains here the commonplace, the ordinary, even old fashioned that stubbornly refuses to let go of the past, or simply remains unaware of the future. Blended into the day to day routine of many local inhabitants are the customs and practices of years gone. A prop clothes line can still be seen in the rear yard of many a country block while a few chickens forage freely along the roadside. Home made jams and preserves fill the top shelves of kitchens and are shared amongst friends and family. A darts competition at the local pub might find you privy to an old story of snaring game in the high country. And while the mountain cattlemen still ride the plateaus each year, down on the flatlands folk toil in their vegetable patch, wet a line for a fish dinner off the jetty, chop wood and morning sticks for the open fire. Island life embraces all.

The visitor will come as others have done for decades before him to discover and delight in stunning scenery and country charm. A unique warmth and friendliness abound in the Tasmanian people. Those who live here will continue to enjoy the gentle existence the island preserves. With the progression of time the value of life on the island increases. This collection of photographs endeavours to capture many of those elements that constitute the tranquil island that is Tasmania.

The misty outline of Mt. Strzelecki on Flinders Island creates a feeling of peace across this lagoon near Whitemark.

Argo Paper Nautilus.
One of the most beautiful and interesting shells to be found on the Australian coast is often washed up on Flinders Island after storms.

12

Ben Lomond creates the back-drop to this peaceful grazing scene in the Fingal Valley.

The children of Cape Barren Island school pose for the camera. The island has a tiny population of about 70 people.

Mist hovers above St. Columba Falls on the George River near Pyengana while wattle blossom brightens the greenery of the dense rainforest. Nearby the Pub in the Paddock serves patrons with meals and drinks. The surrounding dairy country supports a cheese factory and café, The Holy Cow.

14

A flowering carpet of Mountain Rocket (Bellendena montana) and Scoparia (Richea scoparia) adorns the ground at Ben Lomond National Park in summer. Wildflowers bloom from early spring to late autumn with many species found only in Tasmania.

A burst of evening light on Risby Cove at Strahan. The Gordon River punts were built in traditional style, usually with Huon or King Billy Pine and used by piners along the Gordon River gathering Huon Pine logs.

16

Woolmers Estate on the South Esk River near Longford, featuring The National Rose Garden with over 2,000 roses planted so far. Settled in 1816 by Thomas Archer the property belonged to the Archer family until 1994. With most of the buildings still housing original fittings and furniture Woolmers is open daily for guided tours for a unique snapshot of Tasmanian colonial history.

Dusted with an early spring snowfall Mt Roland, near Sheffield beckons in the morning over local farms. Mt Claude in the background forms part of the same mountain range. With walking tracks accessible to both peaks a day walk will afford wonderful views across northern Tasmania.

Viewed from 5,000 feet above Freycinet Peninsula, Wineglass Bay and The Hazards mark the edge of Sleepy Bay in the foreground while out behind Great Oyster Bay sweeps around to the town of Swansea in the far distance. The township of Coles Bay is clearly visible on the right.

Looking down from Mt Wellington, dawn breaks over the River Derwent at Hobart as the cruise ship Crystal Harmony makes its way in to dock.

Aerial view of the South West National Park. The Lonely Tarns lie in shadow while the morning sun warms the Eliza Plateau and the peaks of Mt. Anne and Lot's Wife. A popular area for bushwalkers, overnight trips are only for those experienced with rugged terrain and changing weather conditions.

Grand-daughter Emma makes friends with Grey Forester kangaroos at the East Coast Nature World near Bicheno.

Snapper the Tasmanian devil, in an unusually relaxed pose.

Jeanette Englefield snuggles up to Daisy the wombat.

A family of Grey Shrike Thrush nesting in our barbeque area. They are commonly called 'Joe Whickies' because of their distinctive call.

The Tasman Highway winds through the lush rain forest of the Weldborough Pass. Myrtle trees form the canopy overhead while man ferns spread across the forest floor soaking up the moisture from heavy rainfalls.

The finished doll is hand painted and sold in local and mainland galleries.

Wood carver Adrian Hunt, in his workshop at The Deepings near Cygnet.

Paddocks of poppies, pyrethrum, potatoes and other crops form an attractive patchwork down to the edge of the sea between Devonport and Forth.

North and North-East

Launceston at the head of the Tamar River in the states north marks the convergence of two large river systems; the North and South Esk along which farming and small industry flourish. Australia's third oldest city, the charm of Georgian architecture and old English trees provide a romantic picture of colonial times. The dramatic backdrop of the Launceston Cataract Gorge lies in sharp contrast to the rolling hills falling away seaward along the river's edge. Here is the home of the well known Boag's Brewery still brewing from locally grown hops from Tasmania's north east.

Along the Tamar River grape growers produce quality Tasmanian wine. Small boutique vineyards dot the river region offering opportunity for casual dining and wine tastings. Inland the landscape forms a patchwork with the chocolate soil supporting dairy and sheep farming and vegetable cropping under a moderate yearly rainfall. The north east forests drape the high points of the Blue Tier, mounts Victoria, Barrow and Arthur. The Ben Lomond Plateau provides cross country and down hill skiing in winter with tows and accommodation facilities available. In summer the large rocky plateau bursts into colour with the flowering of native shrubs. A short walk from the alpine village allows perfect views along the Esk Valley to the sea.

The seaside resort town of Bridport on the north coast accommodates a fishing port and shipping to Flinders Island. White curved beaches sweeping away to Cape Portland in the far north east are a haven for sea birds and beachcombers. Tin mining in the early years around Pioneer, Gladstone, Weldborough and Derby attracted many with the hope of fortune. Many Chinese came to dig here and became part of the history, still unfolding. St. Helens on the east coast surrounds the expanse of Georges Bay providing a large port for fishing boats unloading crayfish and scallops. Charter boats operate from the bay fishing off shore along the coastline for tuna and marlin. St. Helens is a holiday destination with opportunities for a variety of water sports and the chance to enjoy warm lazy weather.

Ross and Campbell Town along the Heritage Highway inland are superb examples of early colonial townships. Sandstone cottages are predominant in the streetscape highlighted with historic churches and inns. Convict tales are the very essence of the history here. Home to the finest Merino sheep in the world wool growing is a feature of most properties. Northern Midlands encompasses the lowlands beneath the Great Western Tiers. The highland lakes are stocked with trout and adventure in true bushman style while the riverside towns on the plains below are a picture of rural tranquillity. Evandale, Longford, Westbury and Deloraine reflect a peaceful, country lifestyle. Life is friendly and gentle here and the simple way of country living remains unchanged from year to year.

Turbulent floodwaters of the South Esk River thunder beneath the suspension bridge over the First Basin at Launceston's Cataract Gorge.

Rabbits frolic in the early morning across farmland near Hagley. Quamby Bluff behind, forms part of the Great Western Tiers.

Horses and jockeys parade before the start of the Launceston Cup held each year in February at Mowbray Racetrack.

The city of Launceston surrounds the Tamar River where the North and South Esk rivers meet. Yachts and motor cruisers lay anchored in the still waters of Home Reach at the base of the Cataract Gorge. Settled in 1804 Australia's third oldest city has a wealth of colonial history represented by many old homes, parks and warehouses.

The ornate façade of the old Launceston Hotel building in "The Avenue", central Launceston.

A collective view of the architecture in Launceston.

George Street, central Launceston.

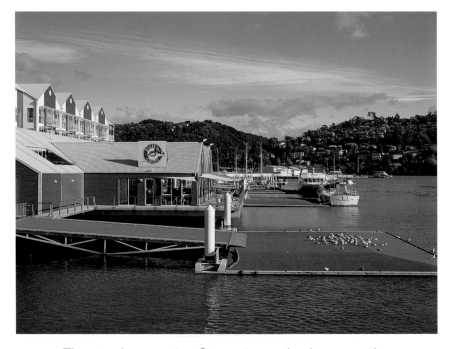

The new Launceston Seaport complex incorporating restaurants, hotel accommodation and apartments.

Dawn at Beauty Point on the West Tamar where Platypus House and Seahorse World are open daily.

Autumn reflections on the South Esk River at Perth, 19 kilometres south of Launceston.

Evening rainbow over Launceston. The regal spires of Pilgrim Church and St. Andrews Kirk contrast with more recent buildings.

Festivale held in Launceston City Park each February celebrates local food, wine and music.

Andrew Raeber from New England Wool speaks to delegates on preparing wool for sale at Rokeby Merino Stud near Campbell Town.

The historic village of Evandale hosts the Penny Farthing Championships each year in February attracting competitors from mainland Australia and overseas.

Artist Michael McWilliams of Perth holds his painting 'Bandicoot on a Log', first prize winner of the inaugural John Glover Art Award. The statue at Evandale, of famous Tasmanian artist John Glover, was sculpted by Peter Corlett.

The Batman Fawkner Inn on the right is dwarfed by the Hotel Grand Chancellor with Holy Trinity Church on the left.

Alfresco dining in Launceston's Brisbane St. Mall. The roof overhead allows for entertainment through the day at any time of the year.

A storm front gathers over farmland near Cressy bringing promise of rain to pastureland.

Renowned winemaker, Dr. Andrew Pirie, with freshly picked Chardonnay grapes from the Rosevears Estate. With 25 years experience he now makes wine for several other vineyards.

A team of grape pickers work steadily on the vines at Rosevears Estate. The cool climate of Tasmania produces a unique style of wine that has carved out a niche on the world market.

The Tamar River cruise boat "Tamar Odyssey" makes its way up the Tamar River past the St. Matthias and Strathlynn vineyards at Rosevears.

Rows of chardonnay vines grow at Piper's Brook Vineyard on the Tamar Wine Route, Rosevears.

Each January the lavender flowers for harvesting at the Bridestowe Lavender Farm at Nabowla. Open daily to the public guided tours are available with a café providing light meals and refreshments.

Harvesting hops on Ian Edward's property at Branxholm. Grown in the north east and the Derwent Valley region, they are destined for the breweries of fine Tasmanian beers.

A thunderhead billows upward as a storm gathers over Launceston.

Bleached white sand lines the beach at the Bay of Fires. Sloop Rock on the horizon marks the entrance to Binalong Bay around the corner.

Historic bridge at Ross arches over the Macquarie River where Wayne French hopes for a trout.

Carved in sandstone the distance to Hobart is indicated on the bridge.

Clarendon homestead on the South Esk River near Evandale is owned by the National Trust and open daily for tours.

Red Bridge at Campbell Town crosses the Elizabeth River.

52

Morning sunlight catches the timber cattle yards near Liffey beneath Dry's Bluff on the Great Western Tiers.

 Grower Colin French checks his seeding onions on his property at Hagley, 35 kilometres west of Launceston on the Bass Highway.

Lombardy Poplars rain gold in autumn at Bella Vista Park Thoroughbred Horse Stud near Deloraine. Spelling and agistment is also provided.

Carlton Cox checking young Tasmania blue gum (Eucalyptus globulus) seedlings, which form part of an annual production of approximately 7 million plantation seedlings at Forestry Tasmania's nursery at Perth.

Grandchildren Jake and Ayla inspect the Big Tree in the rainforest near Lottah.

A moody scene in the iron-bark country near Elephant Pass south-east of St. Marys.

57

At Ben Lomond, Jacob's Ladder snakes upward to the ski fields which open each season with tow and ski hire facilities. Ben Lomond Creek Inn provides hot meals and warmth to visitors.

Shrouded in mist with a dusting of snow, Misery Bluff forms part of the escarpment at Ben Lomond.

Rick Lohrey catches a 3 kg rainbow trout at a private dam.

Michael Poole spends quality time with his boys Marcus and Thomas.

Mark Whiteley casts his line into Arthur's Lake in the early morning.

Moonlight lends an air of romance to this old jetty at Bridport, a popular holiday resort and fishing port.

Owned and skippered by Gerald Spaulding, big game fishing boat, the Norseman III, is available for charter from Georges Bay at St. Helens. Tuna, Marlin and bottom fish are caught regularly in the sea outside the bay.

Eddystone light warns night time shipping of the rocky headland at Eddystone Point north of St. Helens.

Harvested in December, hay on this land near Scottsdale will serve as fodder in the winter months. Mt Barrow lies in the distance.

In the state forest near Lottah beneath the Blue Tier, the ancient rainforest laden with moisture is dense and lush.

Crystal clear water at Bicheno makes this town a favourite holiday destination, featuring good diving waters and Fairy Penguin tours at night. The Douglas Apsley National Park is a short distance north.

Weathered sandstone walls are all that remain of the old whaling station in The Gulch at Bicheno. Today fishing is still a source of income to many local residents.

Summer sunrise in Waub's Bay at Bicheno.

The sea spills over Cod Rock at Bicheno.

Sunrise over Moulting Lagoon and Coles Bay from Cherry Tree Hill south of Bicheno.

South

From the heart of Tasmania beyond the 42nd parallel the terrain increases in diversity. The South West National Park retains most of its natural heritage providing adventurers with some of the finest bush walking in the world. Home to Lake Pedder, the area stretching beyond the waterway is a wealth of wilderness values.

Mt Field National Park and the Wellington range mark the edge of the mountainous terrain with the land smoothing away eastward. Cradled between the Mt.Wellington and the River Derwent, Tasmania's capital city Hobart, sprawls along the waterfront with an assortment of street cafes, restaurants, art galleries and specialty shops. Destination for the Sydney to Hobart and Melbourne to Hobart yacht races each January, the city comes alive with the 'Taste of Tasmania' celebration on the docks. Here is the perfect opportunity for food and wine lovers to sample unique Tasmanian cool temperate wine styles. Locally brewed beer has also made its mark with the South's own Cascade brewery being a popular favourite.

The island's southern forests provide the specialty timbers required for a revitalised wooden boat industry. Visiting the Huon Valley and the gentle easy life by the river one can appreciate the inspiration for Tasmania's Wooden Boat School based in the small town of Franklin. Fruit growers have been harvesting apples here since the days of European settlement. Bruny Island, accessible by car ferry is a place to enjoy boating and a night visit to the fairy penguin colony.

Port Arthur on the Tasman Peninsula is a dramatic reminder of the once violent penal system that existed here. Many of the original sandstone buildings still remain as monuments. The sense of sombre history is relieved only by the sheer beauty of the surrounding landscape. Towering cliffs pleat the lands edge in sensational fashion along the coastline giving way to pockets of bays and beaches edged in soft sand and seaside towns.

Freycinet National Park is a vast expanse of white sandy beaches beneath the weathered rock of the Hazards. Walking tracks accommodate all levels of fitness allowing breathtaking views of the red granite mountains bowing to the beaches below. Wildflowers carpet the ground in the summer months and wallabies are eager to make your acquaintance any time of the year.

Fishing and diving is a feature of life here. Boating enthusiasts will be rewarded in a day's trip with a bountiful catch of flathead or crayfish. The easy way of life along the coast attracts the weekend shack owners and holiday makers alike.

The Tasmanian Symphony Orchestra, with members of the Australian Youth Orchestra, under the baton of Chief Conductor Sebastian Lang-Lessing, performed Mahler's Fifth Symphony at Hobart's Federation Concert Hall on Saturday 8th May, 2004.

Sailing on the River Derwent in Hobart is a popular weekend pastime. Mt. Wellington in the background is accessible by car and provides a panoramic view of Hobart and Storm Bay.

Salamanca Place is perfect for alfresco dining in Hobart. Restaurants and specialty shops now fill these historic sandstone warehouses that line the waterfront.

The Wooden Boat Festival is held along the docks of Hobart's waterfront each summer.

Salamanca Market held every Saturday is famous for Tasmanian art and craft.

The original Post Office is still in use at North Hobart.

Hobart Botanical Gardens originally created in 1818.

St. Matthews church viewed from Arthur Square at New Norfolk.

Autumn colour shows at the Railway Roundabout in Hobart.

The cruise ship 'Crystal Harmony' alongside Princes Wharf in Hobart. The still waters of the River Derwent provide a safe port to many ships including the Antarctic survey ship 'Aurora Australis'.

The historic site of Kangaroo Bluff Fort at Bellerieve gives an ideal vantage point to see the "Star Princess", largest cruise ship to visit Hobart.

Mt. Wellington above Hobart provides stunning views on most days. While snow covers the rocks most winters, wildflowers bloom in the warmer months.

Each December the Toy Run is organised by the Motorcycle Riders Association. Gathering from all over Tasmania at the Derwent Entertainment Centre in Hobart, riders take Christmas gifts for children to Salamanca Place where they are collected by the Salvation Army who distribute them.

The crew of the "Kristy Lee" sell freshly caught crayfish from Victoria Dock.

Spirits run high as competitors in the Sydney to Hobart ocean classic yacht race and the Melbourne to Hobart finish in Constitution Dock.

Battery Point in Hobart still retains many of the buildings from early settlement days.

St. David's Park, adjacent to Salamanca Place, in Hobart.

Dusk on the Tasman Bridge, which spans the River Derwent, with Mt. Wellington behind.

Autumn reflections on the River Derwent upstream from New Norfolk.

The Huon River winds its way through Franklin, where apple orchards cover the slopes and the Wooden Boat Centre teaches skills in traditional boat-building.

Early morning mist makes a tranquil picture on the Huon River at Huonville.

Barry and Judy Price pick Pink Lady apples at Kevin Baddiley's orchard in Huonville.

Hard at work, Jimmy Paul picks Gravensteins near Franklin.

Red Fuji apples are ready for picking. Tasmania produces 55,000 tonnes of apples for domestic and overseas markets annually.

Recherche Bay near South East Cape, the southernmost point of mainland Tasmania

Paul Jager fillets a Stripey Trumpeter on the Lune River boat ramp at Southport.

A Pacific Gull waits patiently for a free feed.

Overlooking Pirate's Bay on Tasman Peninsula, Eagle Hawk Neck has many attractions including Tessellated Pavement, Tasman Arch and Devil's Kitchen.

A peaceful evening on Port Esperance at Dover with Adamson's Peak in the background.

Terry Lean, principal boat builder and tutor at the Wooden Boat Centre in Franklin.

Blue gums (Eucalyptus globulus) growing tall in the Wielangta Forest Reserve.

The fruit of the native Blue Berry (Dianella tasmanica).

A strong Robertson style bridge supports the road through the Sandspit Forest Reserve.

Tasmanian snow gum (Eucalyptus coccifera), grows low in harsh conditions on Mt. Field.

Around 400 years old, this 87 metre tall swamp gum (Eucalyptus ovata) in the Styx Valley, is thought to be the tallest hardwood tree in the world.

The Tahune Forest Air Walk is a 597 metre steel structured walk across the tree tops of wet eucalypt forest.

Manferns grow thickly among the flowering Sassafras trees viewed from the West Creek lookout in the Arve Valley forest reserve.

Federation Peak in the vast South West National Park can be reached after many days of hard walking. Not for the faint hearted, climbing ropes are used to reach the summit.

Precipitous Bluff towers over New River Lagoon on the South coast. The Mewstone (centre) and the Ile du Golfe (right) lay in Prion Bay looking south.

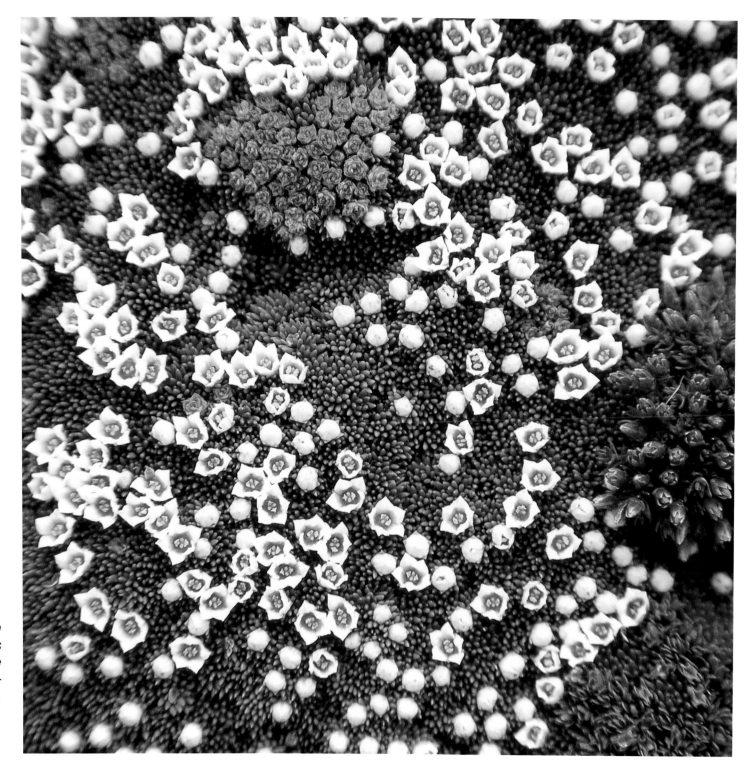

Many varieties of low growing cushion plants are found in alpine wilderness areas of Tasmania. Featured here is the most common variety of Donatia novae-zealandiae.

The weathered skeletons of Pencil Pine trees at Lake Newdegate, Mt. Field National Park.

Geese swim lazily through autumn mist on the River Derwent at New Norfolk.

The sun rises dramatically over the hills around New Norfolk.

On the River Derwent at New Norfolk the "Peppermint Bay", Hobart Cruises new vessel arrives with traditional sailing boat the "Lady Nelson".

Powering through the rapids of the River Derwent at New Norfolk. Tasmanian Devil Jets operate daily for a thrilling ride.

The Oast House casts peaceful reflections at Bushy Park in the Derwent Valley.

The Heritage Hatchery and Gardens at Plenty were established in 1861. Today the salmon ponds are still producing trout and are open for viewing to the public.

Married 50 years, Lewis and Margaret Chaplin's second love is their garden near Maydena.

Burst of light heralds the morning at New Norfolk.

Funded by the Southern Midlands Council and artists Folko Kooper and Maureen Craig, the "Shadows of the Past" project has used sculpture to reflect the bushranging and convict past of the area. Nowadays Oatlands is synonymous with old wares and antiques.

The Callington mill at Oatlands, dating back to 1836, is currently being restored to full working condition. It was known to grind 20 to 30 bushels of flour an hour in 1839.

From the Commandant's Steps the weathered ruins of Port Arthur retain their history as a rigid penal settlement.

A southerly squall highlights the cliff line of Cape Raoul on the Tasman Peninsula.

Richmond historic town represents life from the nineteenth century with most of the original buildings still in use. Antiques, arts and crafts fill the shops where a day can be lost exploring a bygone era.

Built by convicts in 1823 the Richmond Bridge crossing the Coal River is the oldest bridge in Australia.

Prosser Bay at Orford is one of many east coast beaches to enjoy water sports. Maria Island on the horizon is accessible by passenger ferry from Triabunna.

Spiky Beach on Great Oyster Bay is so named for the convict built Spiky Bridge nearby. The Freycinet Peninsula and Schouten Island can be seen in the background.

Swanwick at the mouth of the Swan River is popular with holiday makers. Lining the edge of Great Oyster Bay the white sands of Nine Mile Beach sweep around to Swansea, top left.

The viewing platform at Cape Tourville gives views across Sleepy Bay to The Hazards, Wineglass Bay, Thouin Bay and Cape Forestier on the far left.

The popular seaside camping spot at Mayfield Beach is 15 kilometres south of Swansea.

From the car park at Coles Bay a 30 minute walk up hill will be rewarded with stunning views of Wineglass Bay in the Freycinet National Park.

Richardson's Beach beneath The Hazards at Coles Bay is popular with beach goers at holiday time. The bay provides good shelter for boating and water sports to be enjoyed.

North-West and West

Leaving the Heritage Highway at Perth in northern Tasmania the Bass Highway journeys north-west to Devonport on the Mersey River where Spirit of Tasmania I, II and III dock with passengers and cargo as the primary access point for boat travelers to the island. While most of the population of the region is centred in the coastal towns of Devonport, Ulverstone, Burnie and Smithton, inland the undulating hills roll into forested gullies and peaks and towns pocket the landscape wherever industry or pleasure abide.

Rich, red soil supports an agricultural industry growing poppies, tulips, onions, potatoes and many other vegetables servicing a brisk export business. Synonymous with farming are the towns of Spreyton, Natone, Wilmot and Ridgley. Dairy and sheep farming flourish in the face of the moist trade winds that nourish the paddocks stimulating lush green growth.   These same rains falling in the back country flood the creeks and streams giving life to numerous waterfalls and rushing rivers that course the farmland toward the sea. A journey up a dirt road edged with ferns and forest will often reveal the innocent beauty of clear water cascading in dramatic fashion over rock.

At the heart of western Tasmania lies the Tarkine Forest, Cradle Mountain and Lake St Clair. Picturesque peaks, moist rainforest and cool lakes and tarns form the basis of this world famous National Park. Accessible by car or bus the wild country will provide adventure and panorama for both day trippers and hardened bush walkers. Not far away the country town of Sheffield celebrates the old ways with murals artistically painted on most wall space. Underground, dramatic limestone caves riddle the farmland forming the Mole Creek Karst system, open to visitors with the help of a guide.

Lost in time, Stanley on the coast retains much of its heritage through the quaint houses lacing the town together around a busy fishing port under the protection of The Nut. A trip to the islands lying offshore from Woolnorth historic property in the far north-west can provide the nature lover with more than a passing glimpse of seals and bird life. King Island in Bass Strait like the others is accessible by plane from Wynyard. The Southern Ocean rolls thunderously in to the west coast at Marrawah where surfing attracts those undaunted by the heavy swells.

Macquarie Harbour in the west is rich in colonial history while the terrain surrounding this gateway to the wild rivers, the Gordon and Franklin, is mineral rich. Scenic flights and tour boats offer an opportunity to immerse oneself in the grandeur of this untamed region. Here is the home of the Huon Pine and the fireside tales of the early piners. The West Coast railway, revived from its working past, travels from the naked hills of Queenstown through a thick tangle of forest to the harbour side town of Strahan. From north to west the diversity of scenery will unravel at every bend in the road.

A black and white sepia toned photograph of Cradle Mountain and Dove Lake is hand coloured using oils and dyes recreating a sense of earlier days.

The evening sun strikes Mt. Ossa, Tasmania's highest peak. Situated in the centre of the Cradle Mountain Lake St. Clair National Park the Overland Track leads past the route to the top. Lake McFarlane sits beneath.

Mt Ida catches the morning sun on Lake St. Clair.

Prickly Scoparia (Richea scoparia) flowers in January in the Walls of Jerusalem National Park.

Aptly named, Paradise lies on the slopes of Mt. Roland near Sheffield.

The red Waratah (Telopea truncata) flowers widely across the high country from December through to January.

Blue Sun orchid

Found only in Tasmania, Christmas Bells (Blandfordia punicea) flower from October through to March.

Common Heath (Epacris impressa) is widespread.

Cattley street in Burnie, where alfresco dining has become popular. Burnie provides Tasmanian companies with a freight shipping port in Emu Bay.

The Shrine of Remembrance marks the corner of Reiby and Alexandra Streets in Ulverstone.

The railway line wends its way along the coast line through the Perry Ling gardens at Penguin. In conjunction with the local council, residents maintain the garden beds.

A new day dawns near Paramatta Creek between Deloraine and Devonport.

Workers harvest cauliflowers manually on Philip and Warren Parker's property at Don.

Under threat of a brewing storm, poppies flower across the slopes at Don.

Squash, hand picked at 'Forthview' are destined mostly for Japan.

Uniform lines of cauliflowers grow on Rick Rockliff's farm at Sassafras.

At Table Cape tulips are grown over 17 hectares of chocolate soil. The bulbs are exported to Holland and mainland Australia.

Deciduous beech (Nothofagus gunnii) turns golden in autumn around Lake Wilks beneath Little Horn at Cradle Mountain.

Historic Stanley supports tourism and fishing under the shelter of The Nut (right) at Circular Head.

The naked hills around Queenstown regenerate slowly after years of mining laid bare the soil beneath.

Mark Tregoning gives the "all clear" at Dubbil Barril station. The scenic train ride on the West Coast Wilderness Railway runs daily from Queenstown to Strahan via Teepookana following the original line of the historic Abt rail. The nature of the steep terrain requires continued use of the original rack and pinion system.

Under brakes the train negotiates the steep hills through dense rainforest above the King River Gorge.

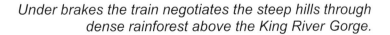

Nestled into Long Bay on Macquarie Harbour the town of Strahan is popular with tourists taking wilderness cruises.

In for a perfect landing the Cessna 185 is used by Wilderness Air to fly visitors in to the Gordon River near Sir John Franklin Falls.

Piloted by Dale Triffett, Seair Adventure Charter helicopter tours fly visitors across the King River Gorge.

Gordon River Cruises vessel, 'Lady Jane Franklin II', at 32 metres in length, sails past the dense rain forest of the Gordon River.

Both vessels, carrying approximately 200 passengers each, conduct similar tours across Macquarie Harbour to Hell's Gates, Sarah Island Penal Settlement and the Gordon River.

The World Heritage Cruises vessel, 'The Adventurer', at 30 metres, cruises the Gordon River near Heritage Landing.

Lake Rosebery near Tullah reflects the surrounding hills with clarity.

139

West Coast Pioneers' Memorial Museum in Main Street is just one of the many tourism features in the now quiet mining town of Zeehan.

Carsten Schwoch finds four wheeled all terrain vehicles are ideal to explore the Henty sand dunes near Strahan.

The Hydro wind farm at Woolnorth in the state's north-west has 37 towers as the first stage. Each tower stands 60 metres high with the blades measuring 33 metres long and generates 1.75 megawatts of electricity. Components are mostly built in Tasmania, with only the blades imported from Denmark.

141

Entering the Mersey River the Spirit of Tasmania sails past Mersey Bluff at Devonport. One of three vehicular ferries the service provides a link to Melbourne and Sydney with several sailings each week.

Information

Tasmania is a state of Australia located 42 degrees South and 147 degrees East. Measuring approximately 290 kilometres (180 Miles) long and 310 kilometres (190miles) wide the highest point is Mt. Ossa at 1,617 metres (5,300 feet).

Tasmania has a population of 478,400 plus, with approximately 85% of residents born in the state. Named Van Diemen's Land by Dutch explorer Abel Tasman who sighted the land in 1642 the name was changed by parliament in 1856. Originally inhabited by the Tasmanian Aboriginal, white Europeans established a settlement in 1803 at Risdon Cove in the south.

Annual rainfall varies greatly from coast to coast with the west averaging 3,200 millimetres and the east much drier with as low as 600 millimetres. The average daily temperature throughout the summer reaches the mid 20's while daytime temperatures in winter average in the low teens. These figures apply to lowland areas with the higher country being cooler.

The Tasmanian flag is a British Blue Ensign with a red lion on a white disc forming a badge. It has remained virtually unchanged since it was approved by the British Colonial office in 1875. Tasmania's floral emblem is that of the flowering Blue Gum, the Eucalyptus globulus growing widespread across the state.

Currency is the Australian dollar and most major international credit cards are accepted. While tipping is not a standard custom when paying for service it is always gratefully accepted. Bartering is sometimes acceptable at markets but not the usual practice within shops or department stores.

Access to Tasmania from mainland Australia is by air or sea. Flights travel daily into Launceston and Hobart from Melbourne and Sydney with several flights each week into Devonport and Wynyard. By sea the Spirit of Tasmania III car and passenger ferry travel between Sydney and Devonport three times per week. The Spirit of Tasmania I and II travel from Melbourne to Devonport daily. Around the island hire care services are available from major centres and bus transport provides links with most city and regional areas. Information centres in most cities and towns will provide updated timetables.

Some useful websites giving extended general information about Tasmania:

www.discovertasmania.com.au
www.discoverlaunceston.com.au
www.tasmaniatravel.com.au
www.tas.gov.au/tasmaniaonline
www.tourismtasmania.com.au

Other useful websites include:

Accommodation	www.jasons.com.au
Bushwalking	www.wildtiger.biz
Fishing	www.fishingtasmania.com
Wine	www.tasmanian-wine.com.au
National Parks	www.parks.tas.gov.au

Disclaimer

Information contained within this book is believed to be correct at the time of publishing; however, the publishers explicitly deny any responsibility or liability for damages and/or losses, direct or indirect, resulting from the reliance upon information contained within this book.

Tasmanian Flag

Tasmanian Coat of Arms

Tasmanian Floral Emblem

Tasmanian Flag, Tasmanian Coat of Arms and Tasmanian Floral Emblem courtesy Tasmanian Government.

Map supplied by Tasmap

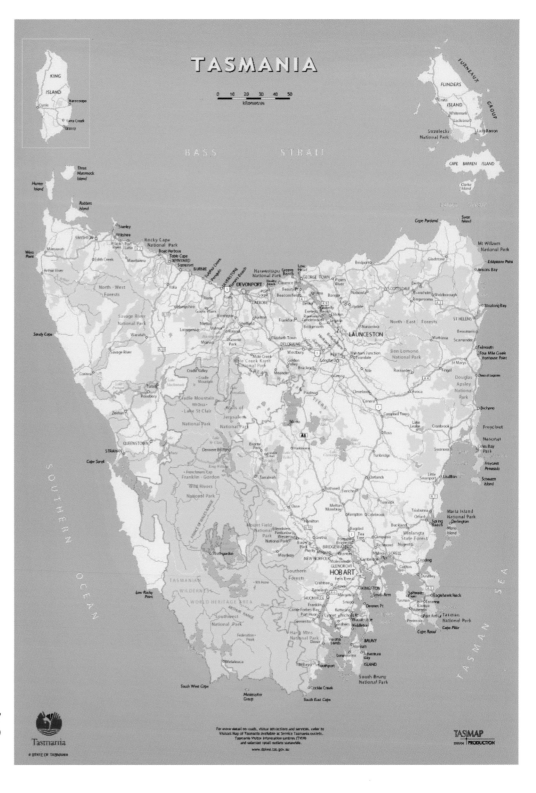